The Cutting of the Orm:
The Secret Calendar of the Priory of Sion

By Tracy R. Twyman

ISBN 978-1-962312-25-7

Originally published with
Dagobert's Revenge Magazine © 2003
Quintessential Publications

In January 2011, following an abrupt adjustment of polar north, the Minnesota Planetarium Society and the mainstream media proclaimed that a new zodiac system would need to be adopted. Ophiuchus, the Serpent-Bearer, was proclaimed as the "new" astrological sign for a new zodiac made of thirteen houses instead of twelve.

But all of this was foreseen back in 2002, by Tracy R. Twyman, then writing for *Dagobert's Revenge Magazine*. In 2002's *The Cutting of the Orm*, Tracy R. Twyman actually predicted that future reform of the zodiac and annual calendar would come about after a pole shift, in which a thirteenth house would be added to the zodiac, and a thirteenth month added to the year.

Perhaps most astoundingly, this prediction was made after examining numerical codes embedded in the literature published by the **Priory of Sion** back in the mid-twentieth century, within documents supposedly written by avant-garde artist and filmmaker **Jean Cocteau**. Following the clues left by this mercurial character, Twyman discovered a new calendar: not one useful for the present time, but one that might some day come into being. Furthermore, the clues also led her to reconstruct the old calendar of **the Golden Age** before the Flood, as it had been before the Earth's axis was tilted to its present state. The results of this investigation will shock and amaze you.

Table of Contents

The Fallen Elm of Gisors

Henry dies, 1189

The Cutting of the Orm:
The Secret Calendar of the Priory of Sion[1]

According to the *Secret Dossiers* of the Priory of Sion, discovered by the authors of *Holy Blood, Holy Grail* in the Parisian Bibliothèque Nationale, the Priory broke away from its military arm, the Knights Templar, in the year 1188, during a ceremony called "the Cutting of the Elm." This occurred following the loss of Jerusalem, in 1187, to the Saracens by the Christian crusaders, who were being led by the Knights Templar, and their Grand Master, Gerard de Ridefort. The material in the *Secret Dossiers* seems to indicate that this was, in fact, the cause of the rift between the two organizations, and that Gerard de Ridefort had committed some form of "treason" that led to the loss of the Holy Land. As the authors of *Holy Blood, Holy Grail* put it:

> The Ordre de Sion, which had created the Knights Templar, now washed its hands of its celebrated protegés. The 'parent', in other words, officially disowned the 'child.' This rupture is said to have been commemorated by a ritual or ceremony of some sort. In the *Dossiers secrets* and

---

[1] [Original title: *The Cutting of the Orm: The Golden Age Calendar And the New English Cabala*]

other 'Prieure documents', it is referred to as the 'cutting of the elm', and allegedly took place at Gisors.

An event known as the "Cutting of the Elm" did occur at Gisors during this year, although the historical record of this event does not contain any reference to either the Order of Sion or the Knights Templar. It also does not appear to have ever been fully explained. Supposedly, there was an elm tree located in the "Champ Sacre", or "Sacred Field" at Gisors. The authors of *Holy Blood, Holy Grail* write that, "According to medieval chroniclers the site had been deemed sacred since pre-Christian times, and during the twelfth century had provided the setting for numerous meetings between the kings of England and France." The Elm was, as the story goes, the only source of shade on the field. It was more than 800 years old, and "so large that nine men, linking hands could barely encompass its trunk." In 1188, during one of those historic meetings between the French monarch, Philippe II, and the English monarch, Henry II, a skirmish broke out between the two men's armies over the shelter provided by this tree. After three days of negotiations, *Holy Blood, Holy Grail* states that a "full-scale onslaught" ensued. The English "took refuge within the walls of Gisors itself, while the French are said to have cut down the tree in frustration. Philippe II then stormed back to Paris in a huff, declaring that he had not come to Gisors to play the role of woodcutter." Other accounts of the story include some other bizarre details. They say that Philippe announced to Henry his intention to cut down the tree, and Henry's response was to reinforce the trunk with bands of iron. *Holy Blood, Holy Grail* tells us that:

> [T]he following day the French armed themselves and
> formed a phalanx of five squadrons, each accompanied by
> a distinguished Lord of the realm, who advanced on the
> elm, accompanied by slingsmen, as well as carpenters
> equipped with axes and hammers. A struggle is said to
> have ensued, in which Richard Coeur de Lion, Henry's

eldest son and heir, participated, attempting to protect the
tree and spilling considerable blood in the process.
Nevertheless... the tree was cut down.

As you can see, the relationship between the above account and
the separation of the Order of Sion from the Knights Templar is
not exactly clear. But the separation from the Templars was not the
only change to occur at this time for the Ordre de Sion. They are
said to have changed their name to the "Prieure de Sion", and to
have appended to that title two subtitles. One was "the Ordre de la
Rose-Croix Veritas", or "the Order of the True Rose-Cross." The
other was "Ormus", the name also given to a Gnostic mystic from
Alexandria who founded, according to Masonic tradition, an
"order of initiates" in the year 46 A.D., and who employed the
Rose Cross as his symbol. The implication is that the Priory of
Sion and the Rosicrucian brotherhood were one and the same. And
Jean de Gisors, the first Grand Master of the Priory after the
Cutting of the Elm, is named in a manuscript by Robert Denyau,
the cure of Gisors, as having founded the Order of the Rose-Croix
in 1188.

The name "Ormus" is itself very suggestive, for the word "orme" is
French for "elm", so the term "cutting of the elm" is translated as
"decoupage de l'orme." But the word "orm" in more ancient
languages, such as Sumerian and Babylonian, means "worm", or
"serpent." Therefore, "cutting of the elm" could be a play on words
referring to the "cutting of the serpent." And the serpent, as I will
now discuss, was a symbol of both the night's sky, and the
alphabet.

The Hebrew alphabet is referred to by Jewish mystics as the Teli, a
serpent biting its own tail, like the serpent Orobouros who
encircles the night's sky, and who represents the ring of the

zodiac[2]. Part of the reason behind this metaphor is that the last letter of the Hebrew alphabet can be combined with the second letter to form the shape of the first letter, Alef. Because of its serpentine nature, the twenty-two lettered Hebrew alphabet is also called a "cable", which is where the word "cabbala", the science of Hebrew mysticism, comes from. In this system, each letter represents a number, the first letter, Alef, representing one.[3] Each letter also corresponds to a planet, an element, and a zodiac sign. The Hebrews further distributed their sacred alphabet upon the Tree of Life, their version of the "world tree" common to all mythology systems, which stands at the center point of the world -- and the universe -- providing an anchor-point for the cosmos. The Hebrew Tree of Life in fact represents the cosmos, with each of its ten spheres, or "Sephiroth" representing an element of creation. And slithering up the paths between the Sephiroth formed by the letters of the alphabet is the Teli, the serpent. This combination of the cosmic serpent and the World Tree is also common in mythology (like in the story of the Garden of Eden). Perhaps this is part of what was being implied in the story of the Cutting of the Elm, which involves both a tree and the implication of a serpent.

The mystical significance of the Hebrew alphabet has become a science studied not just by Jews, but by all Hermeticists for at least the last few centuries. When the Knights Templar invented the system of the Tarot, each card corresponded to a letter of the

---

[2] The Hebrews also equated the Teli with the Earth's orbit. The rabbi Aryah Kaplan, in his commentary on the *Sefer Yetzirah*, states that, "... the Teli is also often referred to as a dragon or fish. This is because it has the shape of a fish, wide in the center, and coming to a point at both ends.

[3] This forms a literal basis for the common saying that "math is the *universal language."*

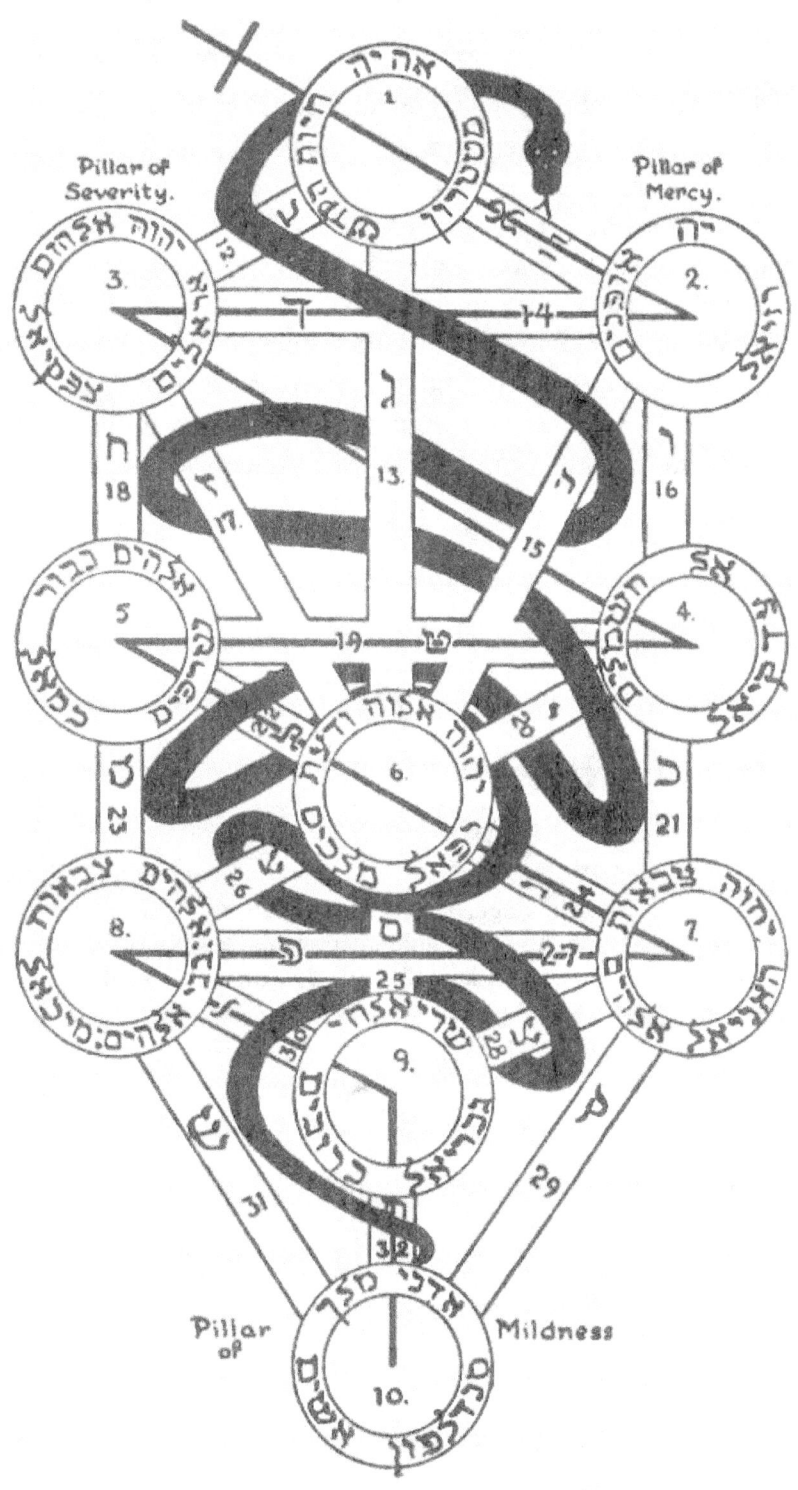

The Cabalistic Tree of Life.

Hebrew alphabet.[4] And when the Hermetic Order of the Golden Dawn created their extremely complex system of the Rose-Croix symbol, the rose in the center contained three rings of twenty-two petals, each ring consisting of three, seven, and twelve petals, respectively. On each petal was placed a letter of the Hebrew alphabet. These corresponded to what are traditionally called the three "mother letters" of the Hebrew alphabet, followed by the seven planetary letters, and the twelve letters corresponding to the zodiac. However, it is my opinion that the story of the Cutting of the Elm refers to a similar cabalistic system using not the Hebrew alphabet, but our modern twenty-six letter alphabet, and to a zodiac system that has been kept secret by the Priory of Sion for over a thousand years.[5] This system was revealed by the discovery of the Compass of Enoch.

This 26-pointed configuration, which is detailed in the article[6] of

---

[4] Note the similarity between the words "Tarot," "Torah" (the Five Books of Moses sacred to the Hebrews, which contain the coded secret of their alphabet), and "Tower" - as in the Tower of Babel that represented the original one-world language. The "High Priestess" card in the *Rider Waite tarot deck* shows her holding a script marked "Tora," standing between the Masonic pillars of Jachin and Boaz that flanked the entrance to Solomon's Temple.

[5] It seems probable that the letters of many of the world's alphabets were inspired by the constellations in the night's sky. Perhaps this is part of the link, consistent in world mythology, between stars and angels. The word "angel" means "messenger," and the stars were considered by ancient man to be divine "messages" written in the sky. It was the purview of astrologers to interpret these messages by "reading the stars."

[6] [Editor: *13: Secret Power, Sacred Number*, published in *Dagobert's Revenge Magazine*, Volume 4, Number 2. Most likely the article was conceived and written by Tracy R. Twyman instead of Boyd Rice. Having Boyd Rice name on Tracy's work was part of the publisher's attempt to portray Boyd Rice as being a person of intellectual background. This was to promote the book *The Vessel of God*, which was never published due to Boyd Rice breach of contract by publishing the book online.]

The Compass of Enoch with the English Alphabet, arranged according to the Atbash cipher.

the same name by Boyd Rice, provides an obvious number correspondence for each letter of the alphabet, although it does not merely go in chronological order, with A being 1 and Z being 26. When the alphabet is placed upon the Compass of Enoch according to certain clues which I have discovered, it is split in half at the M, and then the rest is turned backwards, mirroring the first half in perfect symmetry, giving Z the value of 14, and N the value of 26. Therefore, A is on the opposite side of the wheel to Z, showing a reflective relationship between the "Alpha and Omega," the beginning and the end. Between the letters zigzags a continuous line that connects each letter to its opposite. This line is the equivalent of the Teli serpent -- the Orm -- which encompasses the Hebrew alphabet, and the zigzagging is similar to the way in which the Serpent of Wisdom zigzags its way up the Tree of Life in the Hebrew cabala, while the lightening-bolt-like "Flaming Sword" of divine light zigzags its way down the tree. Significantly, the reason why the serpent zigzags in this fashion is exactly because the alphabet has been cut at the M.[7] Is this division of the alphabet what the "Cutting of the Elm" story is supposed to signify? The title "Ormus" that the Priory of Sion took on after the Cutting of the Elm was written with the letters "O," "R," "U," and "S," placed inside of the middle letter, "M," which was written like the astrological symbol for Virgo - a sign that resembles an M combined with an Ichthys fish symbol. Later on, the Priory also took possession of a relic that had gotten the Knights Templar in a lot of trouble - a skull named Baphomet, also called by the title "Caput 58M," with the M written as the Virgo sign. Now since M is the thirteenth letter of the alphabet, and five plus eight equals thirteen, it has been speculated that this was a code for "MM" - "Mary Magdalene," and that the skull which the Templars possessed was hers. Logical. But in another sense, it could also be a code for this particular cipher system. Thirteen plus thirteen is

---

[7] In the Bible, the dragon Leviathan, which clearly represents the celestial snake, is specifically called "the Crooked Serpent."

twenty-six, i.e., the twenty-six letters of the alphabet, which, on the Compass of Enoch, is split at the thirteenth letter, the M. And the Compass of Enoch also creates a geometric shape that includes a pattern of thirteen oblong Ms.[8]

Virgo

The number thirteen is very important in the occult, but especially to the Freemasons, the Knights Templar, and the Merovingians. The Templars were arrested in France on Friday, October 13th, which thereafter gave rise to the superstition that Friday the 13th was an unlucky day. Their symbol of the skull and crossbones was the basis for the "Jolly Roger" flag used by pirates (many of them Freemasons), which features, underneath the symbol, the number thirteen.[9] The Merovingian bloodline and its offshoots are called by conspiracy theorists "the 13th Illuminati bloodline," and the Grail-related magical order from the 14th century known as the Dragon Court, consisted, according to author Nicholas de Vere in

---

[8] Since Magdalene's name means "Tower," she would seem to represent the alphabet itself, further signified by the Tower of Babel. (This may also link up to the fact that the "houses" of the zodiac are split up into four sections, each dedicated to a cardinal point, which are called "watchtowers.") In this light, it is significant that Berenger Saunière built a tower on his property dedicated to her in which he housed his *library*. He also repeatedly encoded references to the number twenty-two, the number of letters in the Hebrew alphabet.

[9] The number thirteen itself is considered so baleful that there is actually a name -- triskaidekaphobia -- for the psychological condition of the fear of 13. This is why so many buildings, especially on the East Coast of the United States, do not have a thirteenth floor.

The Dragon Legacy: The Secret History of an Ancient Bloodline, of "twenty-six members, or two magical circles of 13." The number thirteen is also integral to the founding of the United States, which began with thirteen colonies that turned into the first thirteen states, and which were represented on our first flag as thirteen hexagonal stars. (These stars were later changed to pentagonal shapes.) The number thirteen is all over our one-dollar bill also, on the Great Seal of the United States, created by Freemasons, who founded this country. On the backside of the seal, there is an eagle holding thirteen arrows, and an olive branch with thirteen leaves. His shield contains thirteen stripes, and above his head are thirteen pentagon stars made in the shape of a hexagram. In his mouth he holds a banner that says "E Pluribus Unum" - "Out of Many, One" - a phrase containing thirteen letters. The number "One," or "1" is also written on the dollar twelve times, unless you count the Latin word "Unum," which would make thirteen. On the front side of the Great Seal are the words "Annuit Coeptis" and "Novus Ordo Secorlum." The phrase "Annuit Coeptis" contains, again, thirteen letters, and is usually translated, "He [meaning 'God'] agrees with the cause which we have started."

However, this translation appears to have no basis in reality. All one needs is a simple Latin dictionary. "Annuit" means "circuit" - like the circuit of the zodiac in the night's sky, and the precession of the equinox. This meaning is further encoded into the word "Annuit" itself. "Annu" relates to "Anno," which means "circle," and "year," while "Nuit" means "night" in French, and is related to the Egyptian word for night, "Nut." The word "Coeptis" means "new beginning." This goes along well with the words at the bottom, "Novus Ordo Seclorum," which mean "New World Order." So the statement being made here is, perhaps, that at the beginning of the new astrological age -Aquarius -- we will have a new secular order on Earth, symbolized by the eye and the pyramid. The dawn of this new age is symbolized by the tale of the death of the last Merovingian king, Dagobert II, during a hunting trip taking place on December 23. Since "Dag" means "fish," and "Bert" means "house," this symbolizes the death of the "fish house," the Age of Pisces, at the dawning of the Age of Aquarius. Interestingly, the Mayan calendar, which is based largely on the number thirteen, ends on December 23, 2012, right on the brink of the Age of Aquarius, and on the anniversary of Dagobert's death.

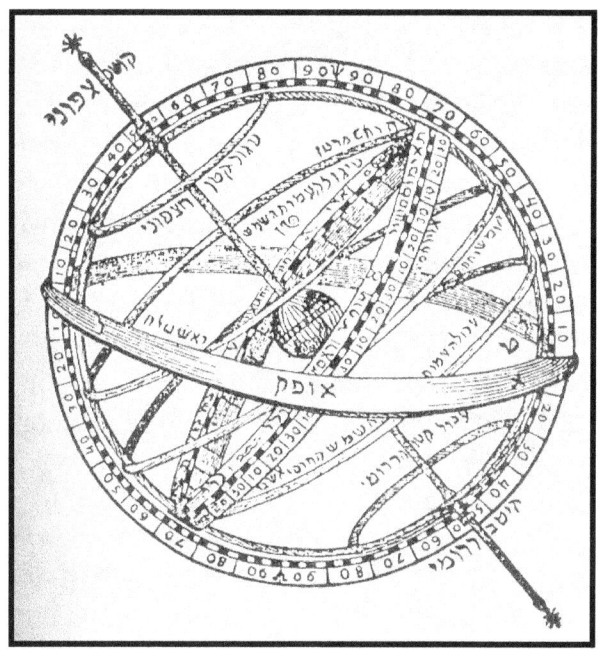

The Hebrew alphabet placed upon the Zodiac.

It was at this point in the investigation that I had a major flash of insight. In the magazine called *CIRCUIT*, published in the forties and fifties by the Priory of Sion, they describe a thirteen-house zodiac system,[10] with the insertion of the constellation of

---

[10] One of the illustrations in the Priory of Sion publication *Vaincre* depicted a man mounted upon a white horse and bearing a flag of the

Ophiuchus - "the Serpent-Holder," constituting the extra house. They also published a poem called *Le Serpent Rouge* (*The Red Serpent*), written, it would appear, by their Grand Master, Jean Cocteau. This poem consisted of thirteen stanzas, each dedicated to one of these zodiac houses, starting with Aquarius and ending with Capricorn, the sign under which Dagobert was killed. Here we have two very distinct references to the zodiac and the serpent. Ophiuchus, the Serpent-Holder, was the constellation that traditionally rules over the science of medicine, just like Mercury. It therefore makes sense that Ophiuchus would be a zodiacal representation of Mercury, and should be symbolized, just like the god and planet Mercury, by the caduceus, a winged staff intertwined with two serpents. It occurred to this author that the serpent of the thirteen-house zodiac could be equated with the implied serpent, or Orm, of the Compass of Enoch, and the twenty-six-letter alphabet could be applied to this thirteen-house system, with two letters assigned to each house. Since there was so much emphasis in the clues to the Grail mystery equating the sign of Virgo with the letter M, it made sense to make that one of Virgo's letters on the wheel. And that, at least, gave me a starting point with which to orient the rest of the zodiac on the compass.

Just a day or so later, the next breakthrough occurred. In Chapter Eight of *Holy Blood, Holy Grail*, the structure of the Priory of Sion is examined in detail. According to the statutes published in *Secret Dossiers* prior to 1956, the order consisted of seven grades, with a total of 1093 members, whereas the post-1956 statutes had it broken down into nine grades, totaling 9841 members. In addition, a set of twenty-two statutes written and signed by Grand Master Jean Cocteau describes a structure of five grades. However, in all three versions of the structure, the number of members in each grade is three times larger than the number of members in the next grade, and all of the numbers, except for one

---

"United States of Europe" riding towards a sunset, upon which was inscribed the sign for Aquarius.

1 and 3, are divisible by nine. It would appear that the only difference between the three versions of the structure is that the pre-1956 statutes are not counting the members of the lowest two grades. Also, the Jean Cocteau statutes have one-third as many people listed in each grade, with 243 members of a fourth grade that are considered part of an outer order, or laity, called the "Children of Saint Vincent." They were created, say the statutes, in 1681 - a very important date to the Rennes-le-Chateau mystery.

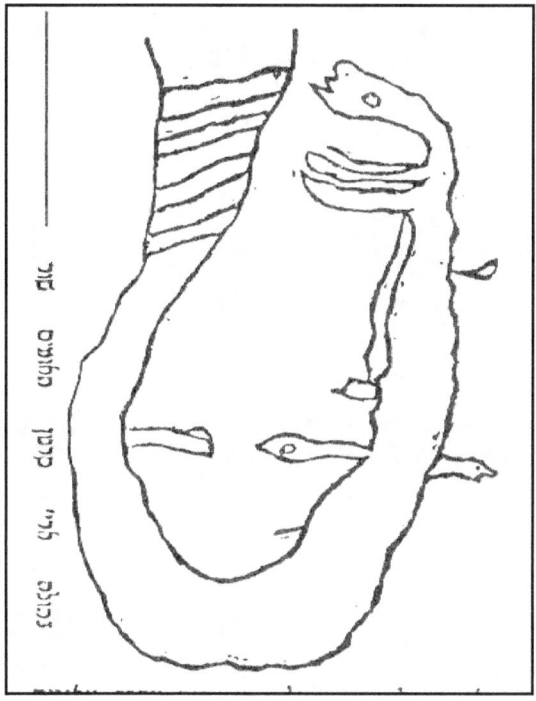

The Teli serpent.

In the post-1956 statutes, the structure is also broken down into provinces (each of which contains forty members), commanderies, and the "Arch Kyria," the name for the top three grades, which consists of a total of thirteen members. The structure, as quoted from the *Secret Dossiers*, is as follows:

The general assembly consists of all members of the association. It consists of 729 provinces, 27 commanderies, and an Arch designated 'Kyria.'

Each of the commanderies, as well as the arch, must consist of forty members, each province of thirteen members.

The members compose a hierarchy of **9** grades.

a) in the **729** provinces
1) Novices: **6, 561** members
2) Croises de Saint-Jean: **2,187**

b) in the **27** commanderies
3) Preux: **729** members
4) Ecuyers: **243** members
5) Chevalieres: **81** members
6) Commandeurs: **27**

c) in the Arch 'Kyria':
7) Connetables: **9** members
8) Senechaux: **3** members
9) Nautonnier: **1** members

Meanwhile, the statutes written by Jean Cocteau state the following:

The hierarchy of the Prieure de Sion is composed of five grades:

1st Nautonnier, number: **1**
2nd Croise, number: **3**
3rd Commandeur, number: **9**
4th Chevalier, number: **27**
5th, Ecuyer, number: **81**
total number :**121**

The first two levels are part of a substructure called 'The Arch of the **13** Rose-Croix.'

The other levels are part of a substructure called 'The **9** commanderies of the Temple.'

In addition, Article 19 states that:

There are **243** Free Brothers, called 'Preux', or, since the year **1681**, Enfants de Saint Vincent, who participate neither in the vote, nor in the Convents, but to whom the Prieure accords certain rights and privileges, in conformity with the decree of **January 17, 1681**.

While most of the numbers here are, as I have stated, divisible by nine, the total number of members according to each version of the statutes is not. However, attempting to divide them by nine reveals some interesting relationships. For instance, the total number of members, according to the post-1956 statues, is 9841. 9841/9 = 1093.44444... - the same number, minus the decimals, as the number of members according to the pre-1956 statutes. 1093/9 = 121.44444... - the same number, minus the decimals, as the number of dignitaries (ranked members) according to the Cocteau statutes. 364, the number of total members according to Cocteau, including the 243 Children of Saint Vincent, when divided by nine, gives us 40.44444... - the same number, minus the decimals, as the number of members in each commanderie. And 121/9 = 13.44444... - the same number, minus the decimals, as the number of members in the "Arch Kyria," or "Arch of the Thirteen Rose-Croix."

Thirteen. There's that number again. It occurred to me that the "Thirteen Rose-Croix" might relate to the cabala of the modern alphabet implied by the Compass of Enoch, and that this shape might, in fact, play the same role as the rose cross which contains the twenty-two letters of the Hebrew alphabet in the Hebrew

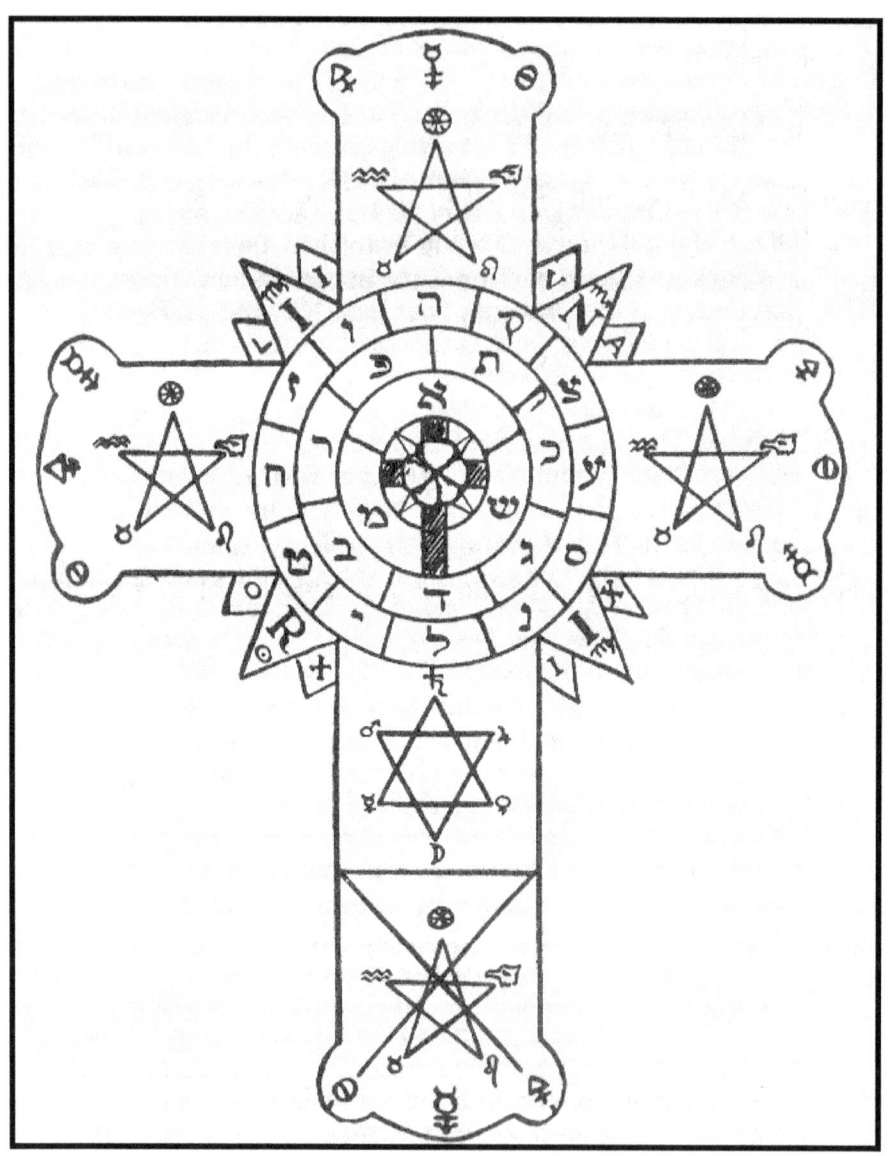

The Rose-Cross lamen with the Hebrew alphabet in the center.

cabala. It could be considered a "thirteen-petaled rose" containing the twenty-six letters of our modern alphabet. Thirteen-petaled flowers do occur in nature, and include the globe flower, ragwort, double delphiniums, mayweed, corn, marigold, and chamomile. The average number of petals on each type of flower are always Fibonacci numbers, a number sequence - discussed later in this article and in other *Dagobert's Revenge* articles - that reflects the growth pattern of nature, and which includes the number thirteen. Interestingly, Stan Tenen (a theoretical physicist whose pet theory is that all ancient alphabets were based upon the Fibonacci spiral) refers in one of his lectures to a structure which he calls the "thirteen-petaled rose," a set of twelve spheres arranged around a thirteenth sphere, which is the most compact three-dimensional structure possible, and which occurs repeatedly in nature. Also, the royal esoteric symbol known as the Tudor Rose sometimes contains an inner circle of five petals, and an outer circle of eight, for a total of thirteen. The hypothesis of the "Thirteen Rose-Croix," then, would appear to be a distinct possibility.

But still I wondered: How might these numbers from the Priory of Sion relate to the thirteen-house zodiac? I decided to subtract thirteen from each of the numbers that would not divide evenly by nine, and then try the division again:

$9841 - 13 = 9828$
$9828/9 = 1092$ (just one less than 1093)

$1093 - 13 = 1080$
$1080/9 = 120$ (just one less than 121)

$121 - 13 = 108$
$108/9 = 12$ (just one less than 13)

and:

364-13 = 351
351/9 = 39 (just one less than 40)
And 39 is also 3 x 13

Then I noticed another thing:

1+0+9+3 = 13

and:

3+6+4 = 13

But even more astounding:

364/13 = 28

It was at this point that the meaning encoded in the number structure of the Priory of Sion came flooding into my mind. 28 is the average number of days in a lunar cycle, and there are thirteen lunar cycles in a solar year, making the 364-day lunar calendar observed by some of our ancestors, with thirteen months of exactly 28 days each. 364 is the exact number of days it takes for the Moon to travel through the zodiac.[11] Also, 364 is very close to the number of days (365.2424) in our current solar year. Throwing caution to the wind, I decided to speculate: What would happen if we actually did observe a 364-day calendar? What would happen if, at some time in the past, the solar year had corresponded precisely with the lunar year?

The answer is that then we could have a perfect calendar, consisting of thirteen months of 28 days, each dedicated to one of the thirteen houses of the zodiac. Also, we could still have 7 days in a week, *exactly* four weeks in each month, and *exactly* 52 weeks in each year. In our current system, the number of weeks in a

---

[11] 28 is an interesting number because it is the sum of the numbers 1-7, and is equal to the sum of its divisors (1+2+4+7+14 = 28).

month, and in a year, is neither exact nor consistent. But in this system, all months would begin and end on the same day of the week, and would match each other perfectly. All floating holidays, such as Thanksgiving and Easter, would occur on the same day every year. The menstrual cycle of each woman would begin on the same day and end on the same day of each month, also making periods of high fertility easier to calculate.[12] Since each zodiac sign would correspond to a single month, all zodiac periods would be of equal length, with no "cusps," and everyone could easily determine which sign a person was born under simply by knowing the month of their birth. One could even break down the hours in a day into a thirteen-based system. We could split the day into twenty-six hours, each consisting of fifty-two minutes, which would in turn consist of fifty-two seconds each. That would give you a total of 25, 590, 656 seconds in a year.

For thousands of years, men have been trying to create an "aliquot calendar," a perfect system that would synthesize both the solar and lunar cycles with exact, whole numbers. But as Duncan Steel remarks in *Marking Time: The Epic Quest to*

---

[12] We should presume that calculating these menstrual cycles would have been something that was very important to the "Grail kings" of the ancient world, especially if, as author Nicholas de Vere von Drakenberg claims, they drew wisdom and power from a vampire ritual that involved drinking the menstrual blood of "Grail maidens" to obtain the blood's melatonin-rich essences, which De Vere terms "starfire." An interesting myth pertaining to the symbolism of the World Tree encoiled with a serpent illustrates the importance of the menstrual cycle and the number 13. As De Vere writes in his book *The Dragon Legacy: The Secret History of an Ancient Bloodline*: "Yggdrasil, the Tree of Life of the Viking kabala or Nine Worlds system, is coiled about at its base by the serpent-dragon Jormungr the Encircler. At Yggdrasil's roots there is a pool. In Ireland, Scotland and Wales, this symbol is repeated as the Hazel Tree by the Well, in which lives the Salmon of Knowledge. Atop the branches of the Hazel tree there sits an eagle who drops a blood-red nut of wisdom into a well 13 times a year. There it is consumed by the Salmon of Knowledge.

Invent the Perfect Calendar, "We have been stymied by the fact that the solar day and the lunar month are not an aliquot part of the year." That is, there is not an exact integer number of days in the year defined by Earth's orbit, nor lunations in that year. However, he also remarks that, "it has not always been this way. About 1.5 billion years ago there were precisely fourteen lunar months in a year, each lasting for thirty-one solar days, but there was no one around to notice the fact and construct a calendar based upon it." The number of days in a year has varied substantially over time, due to a number of factors. One of the most significant factors, however, is called "tidal drag," a force caused by the ocean tides, which are in turn caused by the gravitational attraction of the Moon. This is causing the rotation of the Earth to slow down, making it probable that we will reach a 364-day solar year at some point. Whether or not the number of lunar cycles in a year will synchronize with this at that point is, however, a matter of speculation.

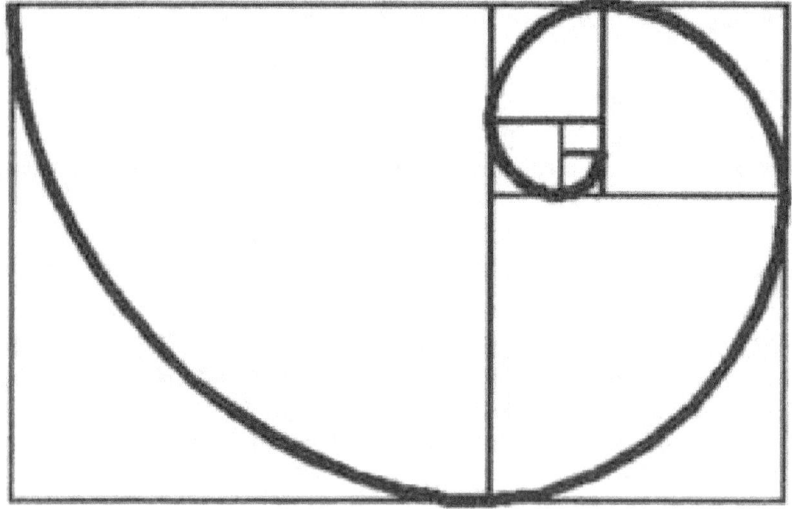

The Fibonacci Spiral.

The Priory of Sion is a secret society preserving *ancient* knowledge, most of which originated during the "Golden Age," at least 10,000 years ago - an age associated with the utopian empire of Atlantis, and the fabled Garden of Eden. This "Golden Age," in which the Hermetic sciences supposedly originated, was dominated by the concept of "As above, so below," the idea that the heavens and the Earth are connected via a harmonious relationship, one reflecting the other, and the idea that nature tends to create mathematically harmonious relationships between all aspects of creation. One of the most consistent harmonious relationships recurrent in nature involves what's known as the Phi ratio, or, more commonly, the "golden ratio."

The Fibonacci sequence is the basic growth pattern of nature. Expressed in whole numbers the sequence begins with 0 and 1, mimicking the creation of the universe, in which the whole of existence emerged as the undivided Monad out of the unmanifested Void. Then, another 1 is added, making 2, the next stage in the creation of the universe, in which the undivided Monad split into the duality of two opposing aspects (such as light and dark, male and female.) From there, the sequence continues, adding the next number to the previous number in the sequence to create the one following. $2+1 = 3$. $3+2 = 5$. $5+3 = 8$. $8+5 = 13$. So the sequence goes: 0,1,1,2,3,5,8,13... This sequence could go on and on indefinitely. When the numbers are divided by one another to form ratios (1/1, 2/1, 3/2, 5/3, 8/5, 13/8), the results, graphed on an x/y axis, form an undulating wave that starts out large and flattens out at an exponential rate towards an asymptote (a place approached but never reached) of 1.6180339..., with an endless series of decimals at the end. This number called in mathematics "the Phi ratio."

In what's known as a "golden rectangle," this ratio can be expressed by dividing the rectangle into one-third and two-thirds sections.[13] Then you construct a larger golden rectangle around that, with the first golden rectangle constituting the smaller, one-third section of the larger golden triangle. Keep doing this for several steps. The whole of each rectangle, when divided by the larger, two-thirds section, will always equal the same ratio as the large part divided by the small part. After you have constructed a series of golden rectangles within golden rectangles, draw a line curving from the inside bottom corner of the larger section of the first rectangle to the upper left-hand corner of that box, then continue that through the larger section of the second rectangle, then the third rectangle, and on and on. This curved line will quickly develop into what is called a "Fibonacci spiral."

The Fibonacci sequence of numbers represent the growth pattern of all nature: the growth pattern of the embryo as it becomes a fetus, then a baby, then a child, then an adult; or of a seed that becomes a seedling, then a plant. The human fetus, the horns of a ram, the spiraling bracts of a pine cone, the whirlpools in the ocean and the storms in the sky also contain this pattern. The golden spiral, sequence and ratio can be found in the visual color spectrum, and in the thirteen-note musical scale. The vibration of each note is the sum of the vibrations of the two notes previous. The structure of a piano keyboard reflects this, with eight white keys, representing whole tones, and five black keys, representing sharps and flats, arranged in groups of threes and two, for a total of thirteen notes in a full octave. This contains the Fibonacci sequence of 2, 3, 5, 8, and 13. The most pleasing pieces of music are those which take full advantage of the Fibonacci relationship, striking a familiar chord with the Fibonacci spiral shape of our own ears, while music that sounds "off" does exactly the opposite.

---

[13] The "golden mean proportion" in geometry has long been known by visual artists as that which is most aesthetically pleasing to the eye, and paintings, photographs, etc. are often purposely constructed with the most important visual element located at the two-thirds mark for this reason.

The syntax of words in poetry, in which some combinations of words are more pleasing than others, undoubtedly follows the same principles.

Not surprisingly, perhaps, our solar system also contains Fibonacci relationships. It is like a whirlpool, or vortex, with the Sun as its "calm eye" in the center, the asymptote of the spiral that is always approached but never reached. Leonardo da Vinci, a Grand Master of the Priory of Sion, once said: "A vortex, unlike a wheel, moves faster towards its center," and this is true of our solar system as well, where Mercury has a year that lasts for 88 of our days, while Pluto's year lasts for 248 of our years. But there is also a "golden relationship" between the orbits of each of our planets. The distance from the Sun to Mercury, when added to the distance from Mercury to Venus, equals the distance from Venus to Earth. This Phi relationship can be found between each of the planetary orbits in sequence, although the pattern gradually breaks down towards the outer planets, while still approaching Phi. This relationship between the planetary orbits is expressed in Johannes Kepler's "Third Law of Planetary Motion," which states that:

> ... the ratio of the squares of the revolutionary periods for two planets is equal to the ratio of the cubes of their semimajor axes; or: $P1 \pm \hat{A}^2 / P2\hat{A}^2 = R1\hat{A}^3/R2\hat{A}^3$

The golden relationship between the planetary orbits was written of in the book *Key to the Sacred Pattern*, by Henry Lincoln, one of the co-authors of *Holy Blood, Holy Grail*. Lincoln's geometric study of the landscape of Rennes-le-Chateau revealed the golden ratio of 1.618 everywhere, especially in the group of mountains whose peaks form a perfect pentagram. Amazingly, the orbit of Venus throughout the year forms a perfect pentagram from the perspective of the Earth, which is why the pentagram is associated with that particular planet/goddess. It is the only planet that forms a perfect geometric shape with its orbit. A pentagram contains in its angles the golden ratio, and from it can be derived a golden

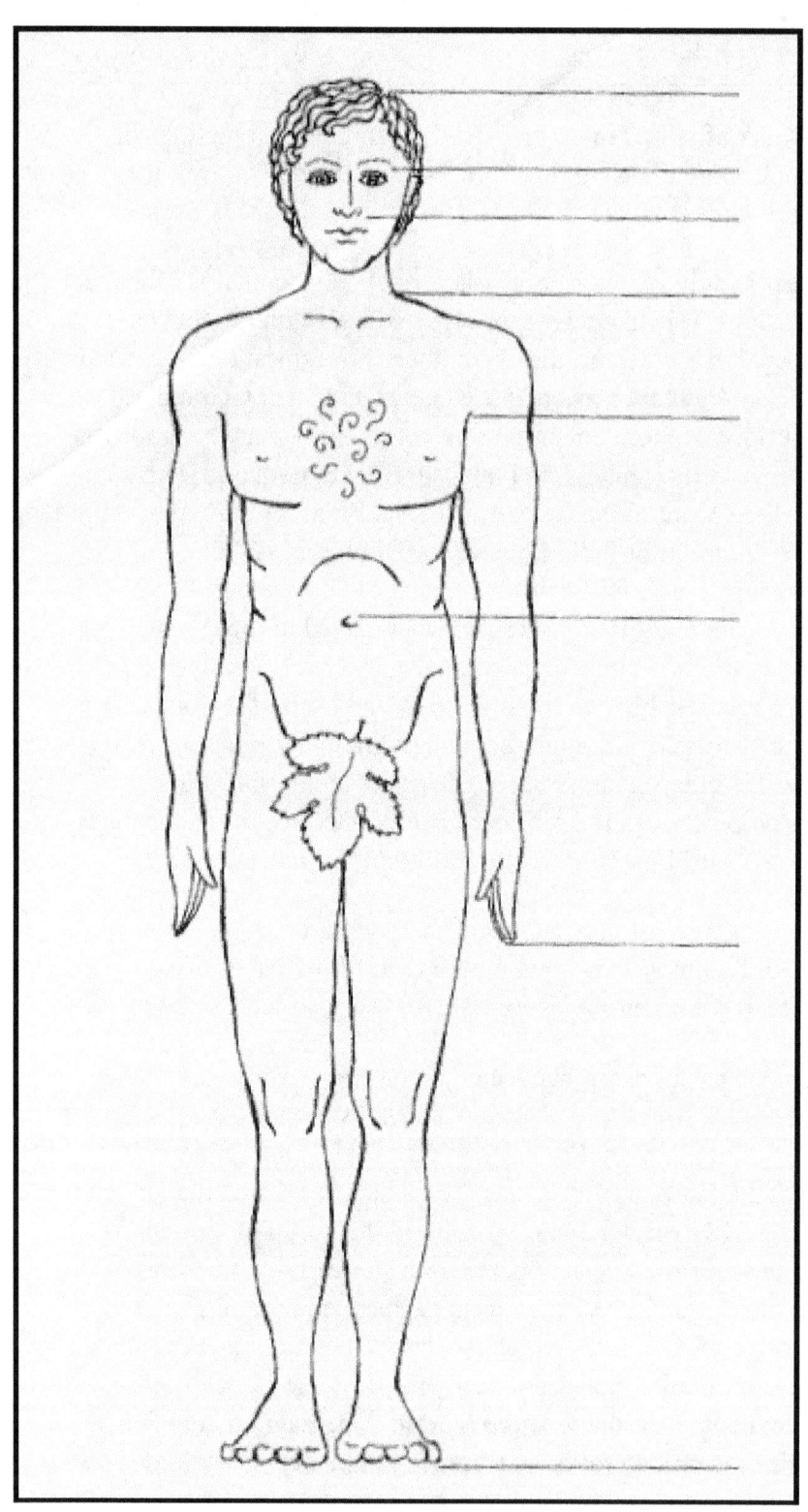

The Golden ratio in the human body.

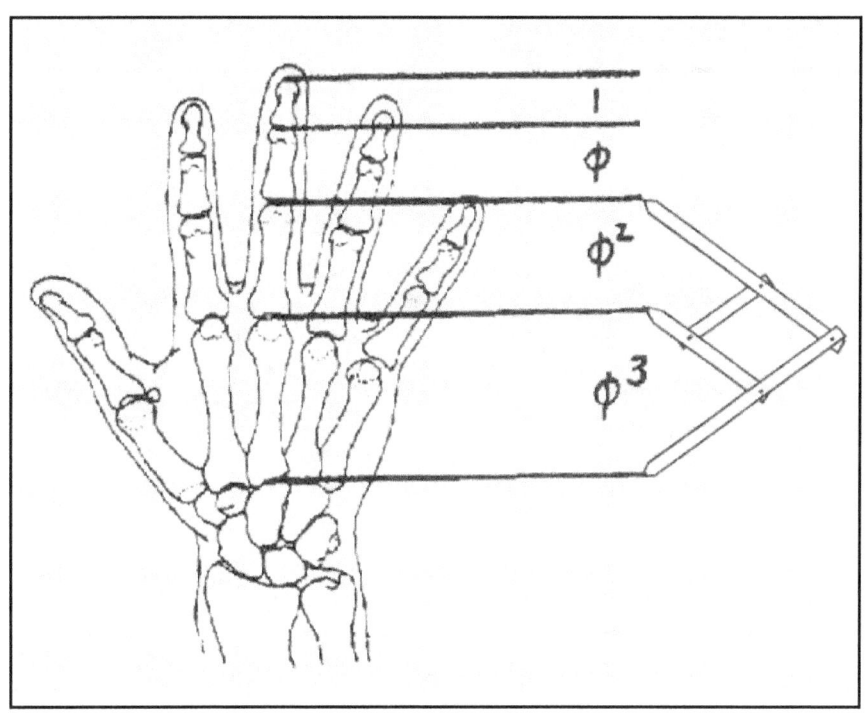

The Golden ratio in the human hand.

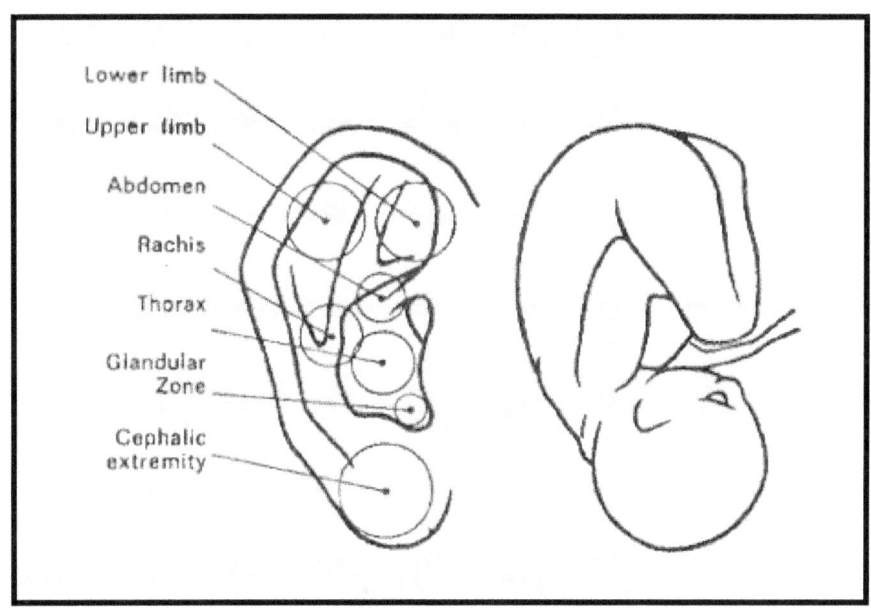

The Fibonacci shape of the human fetus and ear.

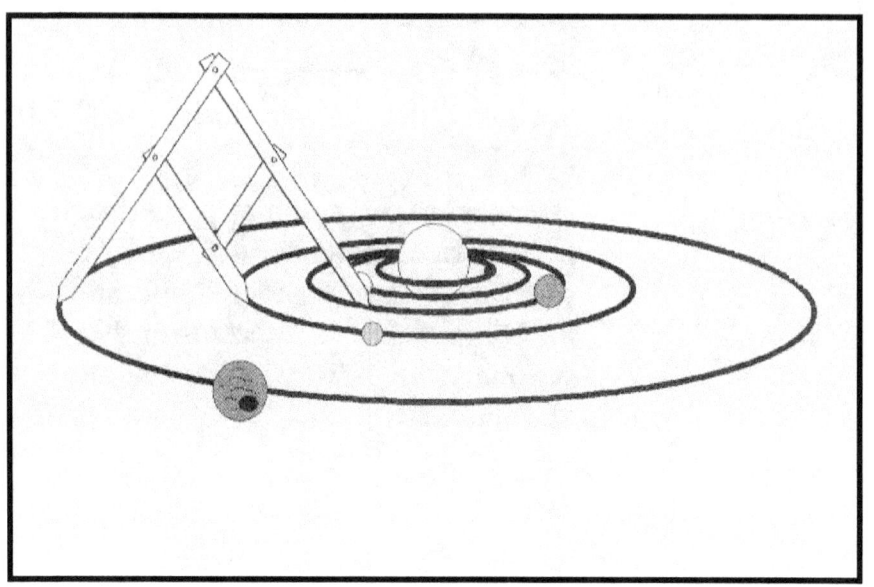

The Golden ratio in our solar system.

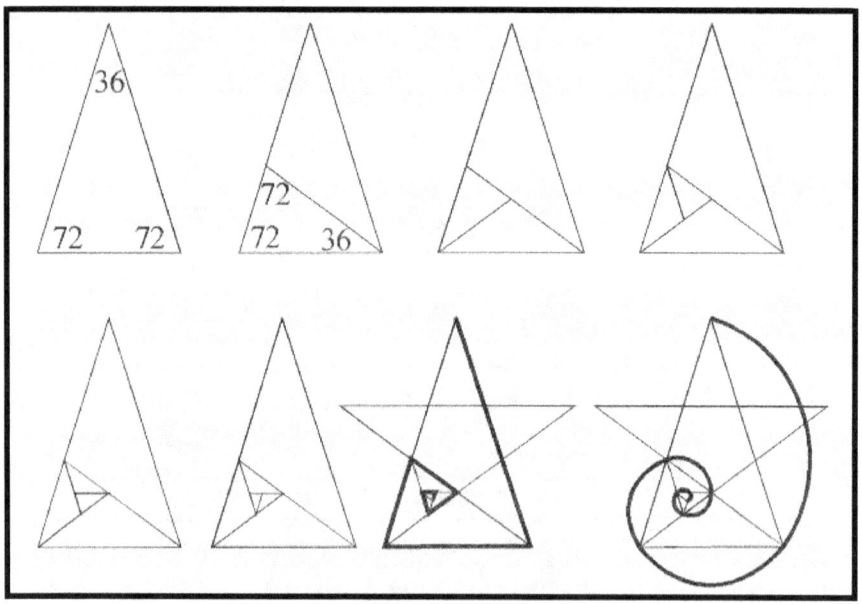

**The Fibonacci spiral forms a Golden triangle
and a pentagram**

triangle. Lincoln, although stopping short of saying that the mountains at Rennes-le-Chateau were artificially arranged to mimic the orbit of Venus, still writes that:

> *The 'holiness' of the Rennes-le-Chateau landscape stems from its pentagonal (and therefore Golden Section) configuration of mountains, which reflect on Earth the movements of Venus in the Heavens. Earth's year consists of 365 and a quarter days. 365.25 divided by 1.618 = 225.74. Rounding off ... leaves us with 225 - the number of days in Venus' year... Venus goes through one complete cycle of phases (her synodic period) in 584 days. 584 divided by 1.618 = 360.9, which, rounded off, reflects the Ancient Egyptian year of 12 months of 30 days, i.e., 360 plus 5 'added' days. Or the 360 degrees in a circle. Additionally, Mercury and Saturn, the inner and outermost planets of the medieval cosmos, show Golden Section relationship in order and size to within 99 percent accuracy.*

Clearly, planets orbiting our Sun tend towards a circular orbit. Venus' orbit is the most circular, with an eccentricity of only .0068, while Earth's is still a mere .0167. As with the Golden relationship between the orbits, the tendency towards a circular orbit lessens as the planets get further away from the Sun. Is that just a property of the lesser gravitational pull from the Sun, I wondered? Or was there some cataclysmic celestial event that may have occurred to "mess up" the beautiful symmetrical orbits that all planets once had, and also messed up the Golden relationships between their orbits? Whatever the case, I began to wonder, for the sake of the perfect calendar, what it would be like if the Earth had a perfectly circular orbit. Furthermore, assuming that the cataclysm had also tilted the axis of the Earth, I factored in the possibility that the Earth's axis may have been perfectly perpendicular to its orbital plane.

So what would happen? Well, as you may have already surmised, such conditions would create a virtual Paradise on Earth, a true golden age. There would be no seasons. The middle portions of the Earth would be perfectly temperate all year round. Daylight and nighttime would always last for the same amount of time every day. At the equator, the Sun would always pass precisely overhead at midday. At the poles it would always be on the horizon. Duncan Steele writes of it in *Marking Time*: "Imagine yourself on this idealized Earth. Each time Earth spins on its axis, the stars do a complete loop around the sky. In essence these form a stationary backdrop against which one may measure the spin of the Earth." Scholars have pondered for centuries how it is that ancient man could have acquired the astounding astronomical understanding that he had, with some cultures seeming to have master the concepts of the spherical nature of the Earth, the other planets, and their relationships to the Sun - things that our culture only surmised millennia later with the assistance of telescopes. But during this proposed golden age, these properties would have been easy to observe with the naked eye. Also, because the day is always the same length, there would be no solstices, just a perpetual equinox, and without the wobble in the Earth's axis, there would be no Precession of the Ages.

Hmmmm.

I had been wondering for some time how the 364-day calendar would fit in with the precession. The number of years in the precession is usually rounded up to 26,000, which is, of course, a multiple of 13. If it did take exactly 26,000 years and we did have a thirteen-sign zodiac, there would be exactly 2000 years between each astrological age. How nice and succinct that would be! And of course, it could be joined with the symbol of the alphabet on the Compass of Enoch, and each of the letters would represent a 1000 year period, two of them then representing an astrological age.

But currently, the precession takes exactly 25,920 years, a multiple of nine, as well as 360 x 72 (reminding one of the angles found in a golden triangle, and in a pentagram, which are 72° and 36°). This is because the zodiac is a perfect 360° circle, split up into twelve houses of 30° each, in which it takes 72 years to travel from one house to the next. If you were to draw a pentagram inside of this circle, it would split the sky into five sections of 72° each.[14] It occurred to me that the Priory of Sion numbers that were divisible by 9 might multiply evenly into 25,920. This worked for 27 and 81, but not for any of the higher numbers. However, there was a much larger number, derived from the precession of the equinox, that *every single one* of these numbers multiplied evenly into. It is called "the Nineveh Constant," and the relationships that it bears to the revolutionary cycles of the heavenly bodies are rather amazing.

In 1857, during an archeological dig in the ancient Assyrian city of Nineveh, 30,000 clay tablets were unearthed pertaining largely to practices of ritual magic. One of the tablets contained a long series of huge, lengthy numbers, one of which was fifteen digits long: 195,955,200,000,000. Over a hundred years later, this number came to the attention of Maurice Chatelain, a French communications specialist who had been studying the Mayan calendar for several years. His theory was that the Mayan civilization had been born of some sort of contact with the Assyrians of Nineveh. In short time he had discovered that the 15-digit Nineveh number was 70 X 60 to the power of 7. He had a hunch that it represented an expression of time in seconds, which

---

[14] The "golden mean proportion" in geometry has long been known by visual artists as that which is most aesthetically pleasing to the eye, and paintings, photographs, etc. are often purposely constructed with the most important visual element located at the two-thirds mark for this reason. Cabalists believed that there were seventy-two languages on Earth that had been handed down to man by God, and one of their most sacred meditations involved the chanting of the "Shemhamaphorash" - "The 72-fold name of God".

were invented at the dawn of civilization by the preceding occupants of Mesopotamia, the Sumerians, and which was based on the 360° in a circle, as well as, amazingly, the circumference of the Earth. Author Peter Tompkins, as quoted in *The Atlantis Blueprint*, by Colin Wilson and Rand Flem-Ath, writes that:

> The Mesopotamians had linked their measures of time and space - in seconds of time and seconds of arc. 34,020 million days is not only the number of days in 3,600 Sumerian precessions of the equinox, but 3,600 tenths of a degree -- consisting of 36,000 Egyptian feet of 0.308 meters -- is the circumference of the world... The Mesopotamians had not only chosen as a unit of measure that was earth-commensurate, it was also commensurate with the great Platonic year [the precessional cycle] of 25,920 years.

Fibonacci spirals of smoke and steam.

When Maurice Chatelain calculated the Nineveh number in terms of seconds of time, he found that it equaled exactly 2,268 million days (more than 6 million years), which is exactly 240 precessional cycles. Chatelain's next discovery was even more amazing, and is best described in *The Atlantis Blueprint*, in which the authors state that:

> *Chatelain found himself wondering if the Nineveh constant was what astrologers and occultists had called 'the great constant of the solar system,' a number that would apply to the revolution of all the bodies in the solar system, including moons. He preceded to calculate the cycles of the planets in seconds... and found that each was an exact fraction of the Nineveh constant...*

> *Chatelain went a step further. When he divided the Nineveh constant into solar years, then compared this with a modern astronomical table based on a caesium clock (which gives the most accurate estimation of the length of a second), he found a slight discrepancy in the sixth decimal place. It was only a twelve-millionth of a day per year, but it puzzled him. Then he saw the solution. Modern astronomical measurements tell us that the rotation of the earth is slowing down very slowly, so every year is getting shorter by sixteen-millionths of a second.*

> *The Nineveh constant proved to be totally accurate 64,800 years ago, and that suggested to Chatelain that it was first calculated 64,800 years ago...*

A hypothesis began to form in my mind: What if the Earth's orbit had originally been 360 days, like the Sumerians believed, and had been perfectly circular? That may be why they based their 360° circle and metric system on it. It also would have matched up with the zodiac cycle and with the circumference of the Earth. There may have been no moon to slow down the rotation of the Earth at that time. All of the other planets would also have perfectly circular orbits, with perfect golden relationships to one another. Then the unknown calamity occurred, which disturbed these orbits. Perhaps it was a large comet that passed through the solar system, bending the perfectly circular orbits with its gravity, smashing into the planet that once stood where the crumbled asteroid belt now lies, tilting the axis of the Earth and depositing the Moon into our orbit. Now, I speculated, the Earth is tending towards a new equilibrium in its orbit, attempting to synthesize the orbit of the Earth around the Sun, and of the Moon around the Earth, as well as the rotation of all three bodies. If this is true, already some amazing relationships have formed: note how closely thirteen lunar cycles divide into our solar year, and the fact that it rotates at a perfect rate in relation to the Earth' rotation, so that the same side is always facing both the Earth and the Sun, while the other side stays completely dark. It is also at a perfect distance from the Earth so that its disc on the horizon appears to be exactly the same size as the solar disc from the perspective of a person on Earth, allowing the Moon, at times, to eclipse the Sun, and the Earth, at times, to eclipse the Sun's rays from the Moon.

Perhaps this event, if it did indeed occur, is what is memorialized in the story of the Garden of Eden. During the Golden Age, the Earth itself was Eden, lush and temperate all year long. Man had no knowledge of hardship or climatic change. Then came the cataclysm, and the appearance of the Moon. This event is synonymous with the "Cutting of the Elm (or Orm)" story, which also involves an (implied) serpent, and a sacred tree.[15] The serpent

---

[15] If the "Cutting of the Elm" is indeed a metaphor for this event, the tree, in one layer of meaning, could represent the Sun and the nine planets of the solar system in the same manner as the "Tree of Life," which the Nordic peoples represented as having nine "spheres" or "worlds" attached to it (like the Hebrew Tree of Life with its ten "Sephiroth"). In that case, the reinforcing of the elm tree with "bands of iron" could

of the night's sky was "severed" in half by the tilt of the Earth, due to the cataclysm, which skewed our view of the zodiac ring, whereas before, the Earth had traveled through the zodiac in a perfect loop perpendicular to the axis of the Earth.[16] Furthermore, the wobble in the axis was introduced, and the Earth began to precess backwards through the zodiac. Perhaps this is why, in the Compass of Enoch alphabet system, the last thirteen letters are wrenched backwards. = The relationship between the Earth and the serpent of the zodiac (from which, I have postulated, many ancient alphabetic and numerical systems were derived) became upset, and thus the meaning of both the letters and the numbers became lost.

This is the equivalent of the destruction of the Tower of Babel, the loss of the secret name of God, of the secret word of a Master Mason, and the expulsion from the Garden of Eden. During the Golden Age, a perfect mathematical harmony may have existed between the orbits of the planets, the zodiac, the alphabet, the musical scale, and the growth patterns of natural life. The Hermetic arts, including astrology and other forms of divination, cabalism, etc. - may have had a much greater utility at that time. The correspondences between numbers, letters, elements, planets and zodiac houses may have been real instead of merely symbolic,

---

represent the orbits of the planets, which resisted but ultimately succumbed to the celestial attack that caused them to become upset, cutting the "Orm," or the serpent of the zodiac, from the perspective of the Earth.

[16] The slaying of the dragon is a recurrent theme in world mythology, from the dragon which Saint George defeated to become the patron saint of England, to the old serpent-dragon Tiamat - who represented to the Sumerians the encircling totality of time and space, and who, according to their mythology, was rent in two by their god Marduk in what is clearly described as an astronomical catastrophe that forever changed the nature of life on Earth. Another recurrent theme is that of a god-king whose body is torn into numerous pieces, such as Osiris being cut up by Set, or Orpheus being torn apart by the Bacchantes.

and thus, these practices may have actually worked. After the Cutting of the Orm, the truth, accuracy, and therefore power behind these correspondences was greatly reduced. But the old meanings were preserved by the initiates, who also set about creating a new system of correspondences to match the newly-forming harmony to occur to the best of their ability. Unlike during the Golden Age, it would have been only the elite of society at this time who would have been capable of understanding the complexity of the new celestial cycles, and their meanings.

In this theory, prior to the "Cutting of the Orm" there were no "equinoxes" or "solstices" to be observed. The Earth was in a perpetual equinox every day. Perhaps this is the meaning behind the emphasis on "midday" by the Freemasons, the Priory of Sion, and other groups. Dagobert II was killed at midday,[17] Hiram, the architect of Solomon's Temple, was killed at midday, and "midday" is mentioned in the parchments found by Berenger Saunière at Rennes-le-Chateau. The French word for "midday" is based on the Latin "meridianus," which also means "meridian," indicating that maybe the reason why the old (and perhaps ancient) Paris meridian is held sacred by the Priory of Sion is because it was somehow the basis of this old, Golden Age system of counting time.[18] The Sun is always at its meridian in regards to

---

[17] The Mayan calendar, which, amazingly, is based on the numbers 9 and 13 as well, ends on December 23, 2012, the anniversary of Dagobert's death, which is known to Catholics as "St. Dagobert's Day.

[18] This could be part of the subtextual meaning behind the battle between the French and the English in the "Cutting of the Elm" - it was a conflict between those who preferred the old Paris meridian and those who preferred the Greenwich, England meridian which is currently in use. Both of these meridians radiate from a central location built upon an ancient holy site, and are the basis of corresponding "ley lines" or "dragon lines" of electromagnetic energy, upon which other ancient holy sites in the surrounding areas are placed. Perhaps all of the sacred sites throughout the ancient world that mirror objects in the heavens -- such as

Freemasonry, states an old Masonic motto. Maybe this explains why the equinoxes were held to be highly sacred days of celebration by ancient man, while solstices -times in which the periods of night and day were at their most unequal -- were often considered to be days of ritual mourning, fasting, and sacrifice. Equinoxes reminded man of the old Golden Age, in which he had been so happy and carefree, while solstices merely reminded him of the tragedy that had occurred to upset that perfection - thus he would pray, fast, and sacrifice for the return of the old equilibrium.

The acquirement of the Moon introduced a new "silver" element into a world that was previously" golden," or entirely solar-based. The Sun is always associated with gold in Hermeticism, and the Moon with silver.[19] The relationship between the Sun and the Moon, from a Hermetic point of view, is a reflective one, similar to the "As above, so below" relationship between Heaven and Earth. The Moon produces no light in itself, but merely reflects the light of the Sun, like a mirror, making it a male/female relationship

---

the pyramids of Egypt, England's Stonehenge, and the Venusian pentagram at Rennes-le-Chateau -- were laid out during the Golden Age, when man had no reason to believe that the stars would ever move from their current positions. The Earth could have been entirely mapped just by equating certain areas on Earth with certain things in the heavens. Note that a common Masonic symbol is the pillars of Jachin and Boaz surmounted by a celestial globe and a terrestrial globe, respectively, indicating a connection between patterns in Heaven and patterns on Earth. Also, the term "dragon lines" indicates a connection between the lines of force on Earth which ancient man used to lay out his temples and the zodiacal serpent in the night's sky.

[19] Michael Schneider makes an interesting point in *A Beginner's Guide to Constructing the Universe* about silver's ancient association with the Moon, writing that, "The ancients chose a symbol more appropriate than they may have known. It was only in this century that scientists probing the atom found that the atomic weight of silver is... 107.870, or nearly 108, a tenth of the moon's radius of 1,080 miles."

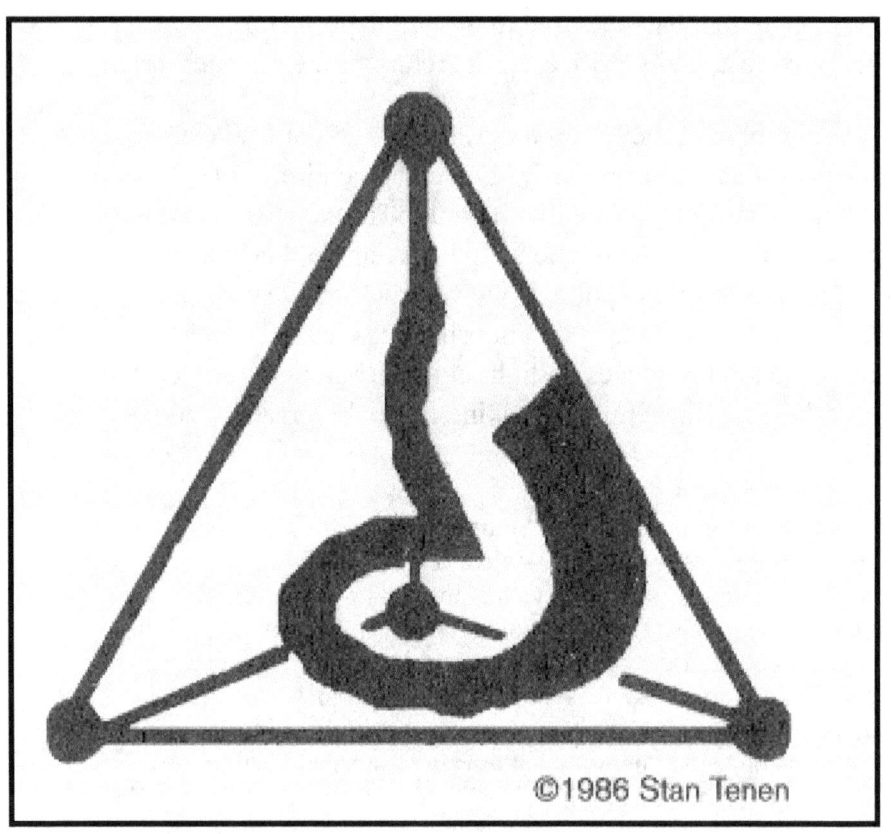

©1986 Stan Tenen

Stan Tenen's "flame letter" resembles the Kundalini.

POS #	# of 364-day years	# of leap days added to the cycle	# of 28-day months in the cycle	Relationships with other POS #s
729	2	1 (728 + 1= 729)	26	364 + 243 + 121 +1 (364 x 2) + 1 9 x 81
1093	3	1 (1092 + 1=1093)	39	729 + 364
2187	6	3 (2184 + 3 = 2187)	78	(1093 x 2) + 1
6561	18	9 (6552 + 9 = 6561)	234	3 x 2187
9841	27	13 (9828 + 13 = 9841)	351	6561 + 2187 + 729 + 243 + 81 + 27 + 9 + 3 + 1
29523	81	39 (29484 + 39 = 29523)	1053	9841 x 3
88569	243	117 (88452 + 117 = 88569)	3159	29523 x 3
265707	729	351 (265356 + 351 = 265707	9477	9841 x 27
797121	2187	1053 (796068 + 1053 = 797121)	28431	9841 x 81
2391363	6561	3159 (2388204 + 3159 = 2391363)	85293	9841 x 243

Above: The chart of Priory of Sion numbers and their relationship to the 364-day Golden calendar.

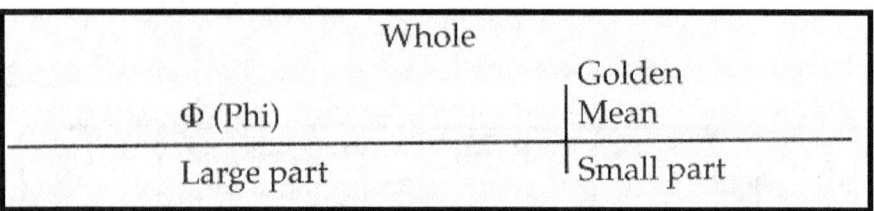

Whole	
Φ (Phi)	Golden Mean
Large part	Small part

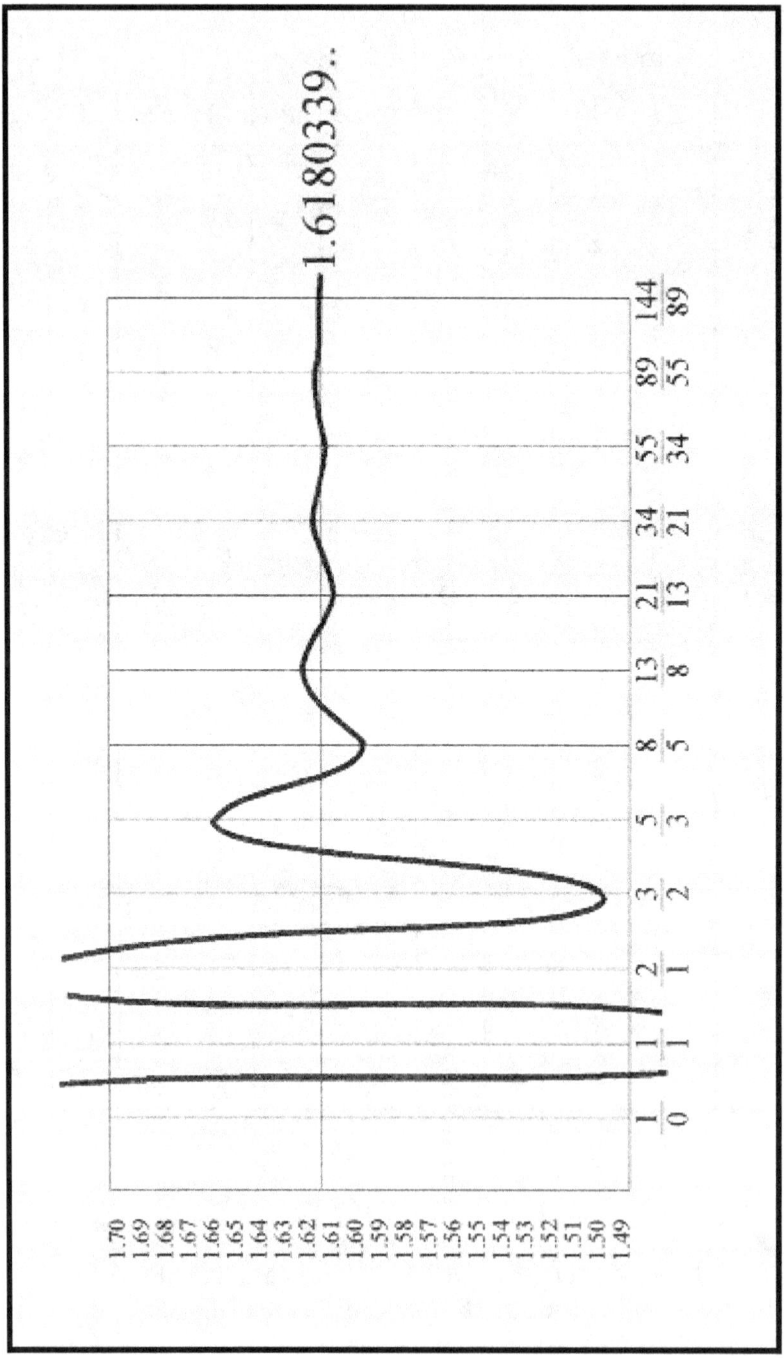

1.6180339..

$\frac{1}{0}$ $\frac{1}{1}$ $\frac{2}{1}$ $\frac{3}{2}$ $\frac{5}{3}$ $\frac{8}{5}$ $\frac{13}{8}$ $\frac{21}{13}$ $\frac{34}{21}$ $\frac{55}{34}$ $\frac{89}{55}$ $\frac{144}{89}$

1.70 1.69 1.68 1.67 1.66 1.65 1.64 1.63 1.62 1.61 1.60 1.59 1.58 1.57 1.56 1.55 1.54 1.53 1.52 1.51 1.50 1.49

as well.[20] This concept is illustrated in the courtyard at the Rennes-le-Chateau church where, at sundown, the light from the Sun shines through the sun disk behind Christ's head on the Calvary, and reflects off of the mirror behind the head of the statue of Mary Magdalene that is surmounted upon the Visigothic pillar. The union of the Sun and the Moon is considered to be one of the greatest secrets of the Hermetic science of alchemy, which creates the Philosopher's Stone, perhaps referring to the new harmony that is now still forming between the Sun and the Moon in relation to the Earth.

With the introduction of the Moon, the tilted axis, and the elliptical orbit, we began to have seasons, with regular periods of death and rebirth in nature. Man had to learn to till the soil, and to preserve himself from harsh weather by wearing clothes and building a house for himself, just as the story of the Garden of Eden relates. The traditionally "female" element of periodic change was introduced, which could explain why the female is presented in the story of Genesis as being the cause of the fall from perfection. Even the word "calendar" has been said to have come from the name of the Hindu moon goddess Kali, associated with periodic creation and destruction, indicating that, prior to the catastrophe which introduced the Moon, and the climactic cycles of periodic change, there may have been no need for a calendar (at least as we currently envision it) in the first place. The feminine moon created the tides of the sea, thus creating the "tidal drag" force that is slowing down the Earth's rotation and shortening the year from 365 days towards 364. It also introduced the menstrual cycle in women, and is undoubtedly responsible for both the pain of menstruation, and the pain of childbirth, something that was supposed to have been handed down by God as punishment to Eve

---

[20] Nicholas de Vere writes of this concept that, "The sun and the moon both represent spirals. The sun's energy spirals out while the moon acts as a vortex, sucking in the tides and the Sun's light."

for her rebellion.[21] The gestation period of a child, by the way, lasts for nine lunar cycles - nine of the thirteen lunar cycles in a year.

There are those two numbers again.

After pondering the possible meaning and relationship between these two numbers, it occurred to me that the Priory of Sion numbers, based on both 9 and 13, are pointing towards this equilibrium between the Sun and the Moon. Nine would naturally be, for a number of reasons, associated with the Sun. The Sun is the eye in the vortex, providing the gravitational glue that keeps the solar system together - a solar system made up of nine planets. Each of these planets contains in its orbit and rotation the nine-based Nineveh number, and these number correspondences occur because of the 9-based geometry of the 360° circle, which is what all planetary orbits in our solar system tend towards. Even the ° (degree) symbol, invented by the Sumerians, represents the Sun. The Moon, however, contains in its orbit and rotation a 13-based system, which combines with the 9-based system of the Sun to in turn act upon the orbit and rotation of the Earth. Aleister Crowley wrote in his treatise on Gematria that 9 represents "stability in change," which clearly describes the masculine aspects of the Sun,

---

[21] After the introduction of the Moon, the number 13 became associated with rebellion. Even Adam's rebellious son Cain, father of the Grail bloodline which the Merovingians belong to, is associated with this number. In *The Pattern and the Prophecy*, by E.W. Bullinger, he points out that that the names all of Cain's descendants mentioned in the Bible, when converted into cabalistic numbers, add up to 2223, which is divisible by both 9 and 13. The 364-day calendar also seems to be implied in *The Book of Genesis*, of which Bullinger writes, "while the opening statement of *Genesis 1:1* is composed of seven words and twenty-eight letters (4x7), the second verse consists of fourteen words, but fifty-two letters; fifty-two being 4 x 13 tells of some apostasy or rebellion which caused the ruin of which that verse speaks." Bullinger seems to make this conclusion certain when he relates that the cabalistic value of the Hebrew word for "Satan" is 364!

while 13 represents "Luna," and "the scale of the highest feminine unity."

The relationship between these two numbers, and the concepts that they represent are referred to rather explicitly in the coding system of the Priory of Sion numbers. This became apparent when the final piece of the puzzle fell into place. For as I soon discovered, the larger numbers, including 729, 1093, 2187, 6561, and 9841, all form a pattern when divided by 364. 729 is 2 x 364 + 1. 1093 is 3 x 364 +1. 2187 is 6 x 364 + 3. 6561 is 18 x 364 + 9. 9841 is 27 x 364 + 13. At first, I thought this might represent a system in which a 364-day year is used, and a leap day is added every two years, so that in 27 years, 13 leap days have been added. This yielded the following chart (see below), which revealed a great many astounding numerological correspondences. For instance, after 243 years (the number of "Children of Saint Vincent" in the Priory of Sion), 117 leap days have been added.

Whether or not the "remainders" on these numbers actually represent leap days in a 364-day calendar, the Priory of Sion numerology system still points most definitely to a mystical relationship between the solar number 9 and the lunar number 13. As if to prove this point, the icing on the numerological cake came to me at last. 9 + 13 = 22. This is the number most consistently stressed within the layout and landscape of Rennes-le-Chateau, as well as the number of letters in the Hebrew alphabet. Interestingly, the Hebrew letter Mem, the equivalent of M, is also the thirteenth letter of that alphabet, and the meaning of that glyph is "water." The ninth letter is Teth - T - and it means "serpent."

The interaction between the Sun, the Moon, and the planets amongst the serpent of the zodiac is what gave ancient man his understanding of time, and forms the basis for the systems of time-keeping which we still observe today. Of all the signs of the zodiac, it was Virgo which was seen by ancient man as being the herald of new times and ages, and she had a very particular relationship with the celestial serpent. A curious reference in *Morals and Dogma*, the classic handbook of Freemasonry by General Albert Pike, relates Virgo to the serpent; the Bull; and to the bee (an emblem of the Merovingian bloodline):

> *A serpent-ring was a well-known symbol of time: and to express dramatically how time preys upon itself, the Egyptian priests fed vipers in a subterranean chamber, as it were, in the sun's winter abode on the fat of bulls, or the year's plenteousness. The Virgin of the zodiac is bitten in the heel by Serpens, who, with Scorpio, rises immediately behind her; and as honey, the emblem of purity and salvation was thought to be the antidote to the serpent's bite, so the bees of Aristaeus, the emblems of nature's abundance, are destroyed through the agency of the serpent, and regenerated within the entrails of the Vernal Bull.*

The GRAL glyph from the parchments.

It is Virgo who was the inseparable companion of Mercury, a figure I have identified not only with the planet named after him, but with the constellation Ophiuchus, because Mercury's symbol was the caduceus, and Ophiuchus was "the Serpent Holder." Virgo also bears a resemblance to the goddess Isis, who is identified with the planet Venus so sacred to the Priory of Sion, and who is described in the poem *Le Serpent Rouge* as being the "eternal white lady of legends, 'Notre Dame des Cross,'" the bearer of the "vase filled with healing balm," the Grail. Virgo is described in the same manner by Albert Pike:

> *Isis, the same as Ceres, was, as we learn from Eratosthenes, the constellation Virgo, represented by a woman holding an ear of wheat. The different emblems which accompany her in the description given by Apuleius, a serpent on either side, a golden vase with a serpent twined round the handle, and the animals that march in procession, the bear, the ape, and Pegasus, represented the constellations that, rising with the Virgin, when on the day of the Vernal Equinox, she stood in the Oriental gate of Heaven, brilliant with the rays of the full moon, seemed to march in her train... The cup, consecrated in the mysteries of both Isis and Eleusis, was the constellation crater.*

Virgo's role as -- literally -- the guardian of the "Gate of the Sun," and the herald of seasonal change -- that is, of time itself -- is further elucidated by Pike:

> *The Celestial Virgin, during the last three centuries that preceded the Christian era, occupied the horoscope or Oriental point, and the gate of Heaven through which the Sun and Moon ascended above the horizon at the two equinoxes. Again it occupied it at midnight, at the Winter Solstice, at the precise moment when the year commenced with the march of times and seasons, of the Sun, the Moon, and day and night, and the principal epochs of the year... At the equinoxes... at the moment when the Sun occupied that point, the Virgin rose before him; she stood at the gates of day and opened them to him. Her brilliant star, Spica Virginis, and Arcturus, in Bootes, northwest of it, heralded his coming. When he had returned to the Vernal Equinox... again it was the celestial Virgin that led the*

march of the signs of night; and in her stars came the
beautiful full moon of that month.

One can see how Virgo, who is crowned with a ring of stars with
the Moon beneath her feet at the Vernal Equinox, is the inspiration
for the figure of the Virgin Mary, the "Queen of Heaven" depicted
in Catholic iconography in exactly the same manner. At the same
time, Venus, as the "Queen of Harlots" and the "love goddess," is
the inspiration for the figure of Mary Magdalene.[22] And like both
Venus and Virgo, Magdalene was the bearer of a holy vase, or
Grail cup, full of balm. At the same time, however, the Virgin of
the sky and the Virgin Mary were both the mothers of the "son of
God": Mary begetting Christ, the son of God, and Virgo begetting
Horus, the son of the sun-god Osiris. When Osiris died, Horus
became the Sun, just as Christ himself came to symbolize the Sun,
dying at the Summer solstice (at Easter) and being reborn at
Christmas, the Winter solstice. An Arabian manuscript in the
Royal Library in Paris shows Isis holding the baby Horus with the
inscription: "I am all that is, all that was, and all that shall be; and
the fruit which I brought forth is the Sun." Albert Pike describes it
thusly:

> *At the moment of the Winter Solstice, the Virgin rose*
> *helically (with the Sun), having the Sun (Horus) in*
> *her bosom.*

One might note that "Horus" sounds like "Hour," "Horo," and
"Hora," and thus can be associated, like his mother Virgo, with
time. It makes sense that it is the Sun, together with the planets
that rotate about it, which are the markers of time's passage in the
first place. Therefore he is, like Kronos, "Father Time." Time is
the great creator-destroyer of the universe, and it is therefore

---

[22] Venus the whore can be seen to symbolize the corrupted state of the
virgin goddess, and conversely, the Virgin can be seen as a chaste
corruption of the love goddess.

fitting that it is symbolized by the Ourobourous serpent, which equates with the idea of death and rebirth.[23] Goddesses like Venus and Virgo embodied this creator-destroyer concept. In fact, many of the good goddess/bad goddess duos throughout the history of world mythology, including the Christian figures of the Virgin Mary and Mary Magdalene, would appear to merely represent two opposing aspects of the same goddess. Note the similarity between this description of Virgo's behavior upon the death of the Sun (represented by the god Osiris) and that of Mary Magdalene upon the death of Jesus, thus linking Virgo with both the Virgin Mary and the Magdalene:

Nine months after the Sun enters Virgo, he reaches the Twins. When Scorpio begins to rise, Orion sets; When Scorpio comes to the meridian, Leo begins to set. Typhon reigns, Osiris is slain, and Isis (the Virgin), his sister and wife, follows him to the tomb, weeping.

Perhaps the fact that this goddess figure was split into two aspects represents the idea that the purity of the golden age was tainted when the Fall of Man occurred due to the corruption of the female element by the serpent, thus causing the harsh seasonal changes that we experience now every year.[24] Albert Pike specifically

---

[23] There are two symbols of death and rebirth on the entrance to the graveyard at Saint Magdalene's church at Rennes-le-Chateau which are noteworthy. One is the Masonic emblem of the hourglass - representing time, and death, surrounded by a laurel wreath, which represents Immortality. The other is the skull and crossbones – the skull of which, by the way, has 22 teeth. The term "Death's head" for this symbol contains the words representing the beginning - "head" - and the end - "death.

[24] People may even have lived much longer during the golden age without having to be exposed to these conditions, thus explaining the extraordinary ages that some of the biblical patriarchs, as well as the deified kings of the ancient world, were said to have reached.

associates the Winter season with this corrupting snake when he writes:

> *The Virgin and Bootes, setting helically at the Autumnal equinox, delivered the world to the wintry constellations, and introduced into it the genius of Evil, represented by Ophiuchus, the Serpent.*

Clearly, this 9 and 13-based system, the Compass of Enoch, and the 364-day calendar that they imply are among the greatest secrets preserved by the Priory of Sion, revealed for the first time in the pages of this publication.

And we can only assume that there is more yet to come. Much more.

Appendix: A

A thirteen-based tarot system using the cabalistic attributes of the modern alphabet can be easily created. Simply take the traditional 78-card tarot deck of 22 Major Arcana (archetypal figures dedicated to each of the Hebrew letters) and 56 Lesser Arcana (four sets of 14 court cards dedicated to each of the elements), then shift four cards from the Major to the Minor set. You then have 26 Major Arcana (each dedicated to one letter of our modern alphabet, with two cards related to each of the 13 zodiac houses), and 52 Lesser Arcana (4 sets of 13 court cards dedicated to each of the elements.) This may be a more appropriate system of correspondences than traditional tarot decks, matching more closely the current cosmic order.

Appendix B:

The principles behind the Compass of Enoch can be used to produce a coding system with characters similar to those created by John Dee from the Enochian tablets that he reportedly channeled from the angels of the Universe's "four watchtowers." Any member of a secret group that knew and had memorized the letter distribution on the compass could then create simple messages that would be decipherable only to other members of the group who knew the code. It works by drawing lines between the letters on the compass which form the word that you wish to encode, not including double letters, since a line cannot be drawn to itself. This gives you a glyph that can then be used by itself to communicate that need without need of the actual compass, or the letters themselves. Anyone who knew how the letters were to be distributed, and how the glyph indicating them was to be oriented could easily interpret its meaning. The reason why these "Enochian" glyphs resemble the Enochian letters of John Dee is because his were formed by a similar principle, with the original letters distributed in English on a tablet according to the dictates of the angels he communed with.

The glyph formed by the compass using the letters "GRAL" (for GRAAL, or Grail) forms a shape that is found throughout Rennes-le-Chateau[25], and on the mysterious parchments that were found there. The GRAL glyph at the top of one of the parchments contains the letter "M", and serves as an indicator telling one how to orient the parchment so as to discover the hidden pentagonal geometry and less obvious code-words which were purposely embedded into it. The same angles as the GRAL glyph can be found in the cocked pentagram in Berenger Sauniere's Magdalen

---

[25] It is also found in the runic alphabet, and in the works of Priory of Sion Grand Master Jean Cocteau.

painting above the altar at his church in Rennes-le-Chateau, inside of which he found those parchments in the first place.